Sandy Donovan

Twenty-First Century Books
Minneapolis

Copyright © 2007 by Sandy Donovan

Twenty-First Century Books
A division of Lerner Publishing Group
241 First Avenue North
Minneapolis, MN 55401 U.S.A.

Website addresses: www.lernerbooks.com
                   www.biography.com

Library of Congress Cataloging-in-Publication Data

Donovan, Sandra, 1967–
   Billy Graham / by Sandy Donovan.
     p.   cm. — (Biography)
   Includes bibliographical references and index.
   ISBN-13: 978–0–8225–5953–5 (lib. bdg. : alk. paper)
   ISBN-10: 0–8225–5953–6 (lib. bdg. : alk. paper)
   1. Graham, Billy, 1918– . 2. Evangelists—United States—Biography.
 I. Title. II. Series: Biography (Twenty-First Century Books (Firm))
   BV3785.G69D66 2007
   226'.2'092—dc22 [B]   2005017999

Manufactured in the United States of America
1 2 3 4 5 6 – BP – 12 11 10 09 08 07

CONTENTS

Introduction: Success in the City......*7*

1 Country Boy.....................................*13*

2 A Preacher's Calling *25*

3 From Pastor to Evangelist.............*37*

4 Spreading the Word.......................*53*

5 Stepping into Politics....................*69*

6 World's Spiritual Leader.................*85*

Timeline..*103*

Source Notes....................................*105*

Selected Bibliography.........................*106*

Books by Billy Graham.......................*106*

Further Reading and Websites *108*

Index...*109*

Newsweek

THE DIET MANIA—A SPECIAL MEDICINE REPORT

Do Fats Really Kill? The Answer

MAY 20, 1957 25c

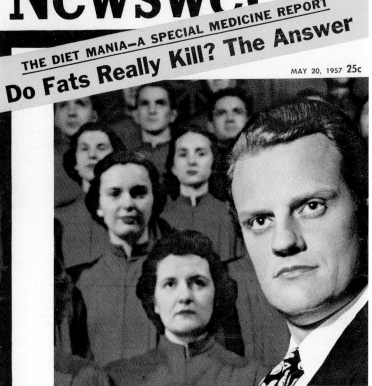

THE BILLY GRAHAM 'INVASION'
Finally the Big One—'Save New York'
(SPECIAL REPORT—RELIGION)

The May 20, 1957, Newsweek cover reveals Billy Graham's growing fame, but it was not his first national news magazine cover. He had appeared on the October 25, 1954, cover of Time.

INTRODUCTION: SUCCESS IN THE CITY

New York City's Madison Square Garden was jammed to capacity. Nearly twenty thousand faces of all ages and all colors shone under the spotlights. On May 15, 1957, this crowd of grandparents, teenagers, young children, sick people, poor people, wealthy people, and others had come to see and hear Billy Graham, the famous Christian evangelist. As an evangelist, he was committed to spreading the words of Jesus Christ by preaching the Gospel. He emphasized salvation by faith through personal conversion. Graham's goal was to bring people to Jesus Christ, and he had been holding citywide crusade meetings across the United States and Europe for more than ten years. Newspapers around the world had written about his passionate preaching and his success at getting people of all backgrounds to commit their lives to Christ. He had even been featured on the cover of *Time* magazine in 1954.

But this New York City crusade was a huge step for Graham. In the entertainment capital of the world, would Graham be able to draw crowds to Madison Square Garden (usually the site of sports and popular entertainment events)? And if the crowds came, would they accept Graham's message and commit

Huge audiences filled Madison Square Garden for Graham's
1957 crusade in New York City.

themselves to Christ? On this first night, the crowd
looked expectant. A fifteen-hundred-voice choir sang
"How Great Thou Art," and people throughout the stadium joined in. Then the tall, blond-haired preacher
from North Carolina took the stage.

"We have not come to put on a show or an entertainment," he told the crowd. "We believe that there are
many people here tonight who have hungry hearts. All

your life you've been searching for peace and joy, happiness, forgiveness. I want to tell you, before you leave Madison Square Garden this night of May 15, you can find everything that you have been searching for, in Christ. He can bring that inward, deepest peace to your soul."

It was Graham's consistent message: people everywhere could find meaning and eternal salvation by recognizing Jesus Christ and committing their lives to him.

TWO VIEWS

When Billy Graham first started preaching, American Protestants had long been divided into two groups. Christian fundamentalists believe that every word in the Bible should be taken literally and that people find personal salvation only through a belief in Jesus Christ. In the first half of the twentieth century, Christian fundamentalists tended to live in the southern states and to be socially conservative: often, like Graham's own family, they did not smoke cigarettes, drink alcohol, or dance. Northern Protestants, on the other hand, tended to be more liberal in their social views as well as their interpretation of the Bible. They often supported progressive social causes, such as granting equal rights to all citizens. Both groups saw themselves as distinct from Roman Catholics. But one of Graham's most challenging messages was that it didn't matter which church a person belonged to. What mattered was the personal acceptance of and commitment to Christ.

In the evangelical Christian world, the term *reborn* or *born again* is used to describe this conversion, when one personally accepts Jesus Christ as savior and Lord. The term comes from the New Testament (John 3:3): "I tell you the truth, unless a man is born again, he cannot see the kingdom of God." Billy Graham preached that this spiritual rebirth, or renewal, was available to anyone, anytime, no matter who they were or what they had done. This powerful message of hope drew many people. Graham had become the most recognizable face in the evangelical world.

Graham followed a long line of evangelical preachers—mostly white southern men—who preached the Gospel of the Bible, considered by Christians to be the direct word of God. Evangelists also invited people to commit themselves to Jesus Christ. But Graham had taken the evangelical movement out of the South and into the rest of mainstream culture. He had already held popular crusades in Los Angeles, California, and London, England. He had demonstrated that urban areas were ripe for Christ's message. But with his New York City crusade, he was journeying into even newer territory for an evangelical preacher. He had turned down money and assistance from the most conservative, fundamentalist New York churches in favor of the broader support of mainstream New York Protestant churches. The move angered many fundamentalists, who, almost fifty years later, still saw Graham as a traitor. But it increased his appeal to millions of

Americans and led to Billy Graham becoming a house-
hold name around the world. In his lifetime, Graham
has preached—in person—to more than two hundred
million people, advised every U.S. president since
Harry Truman, and traveled to nearly two hundred
countries.

The Graham family (back row, left to right), *Catherine, Frank, Morrow, and Billy, and* (front, left to right) *Jean and Melvin, in the early 1930s*

Chapter **ONE**

COUNTRY BOY

THE ROLLING HILLS OF THE NORTH CAROLINA countryside around the city of Charlotte were home to the Graham family since the middle of the 1800s. Billy Graham's grandfather, William Crook Graham, fought for the Confederate army (on the side of the South) in the U.S. Civil War (1861–1865). He was wounded in the Battle of Gettysburg and lived with a bullet in his leg for the rest of his life. After the war, he built a log cabin for his family on a tiny dirt road running between the villages of Pineville and Matthews in North Carolina. Billy's maternal grandfather, Ben Coffey, was also wounded in the Civil War. His leg was badly hurt during a battle, and a bullet blinded his right eye. Later, doctors had to amputate the wounded leg.

Billy's father, named William Franklin Graham but called Frank, grew up on the family farm along with his eight sisters and two brothers. As a young adult, Frank Graham and his brother Clyde ran the Graham Brothers Dairy on their family's land, which by then totaled three hundred acres. Frank Graham married Morrow Coffey in 1916, and they replaced the log cabin with a white wooden house. Their first child, William Franklin Graham Jr., called Billy, was born on November 7, 1918. A few years later, Billy's sister Catherine was born. Frank and Morrow Graham were Presbyterians, a Protestant religion that discourages dancing and drinking liquor.

The 1920s and 1930s were years of great changes in the United States. During the Roaring Twenties, many young people had cars for the first time, which gave that generation a new kind of freedom. Although selling alcohol was illegal during this decade, establishments called speakeasies sprang up around the country. These were clubs that served illegal liquor and often featured jazz music and dancing as well.

The Graham family's rural lifestyle kept them relatively untouched by the new craze. Since they didn't drink alcohol or dance, they did not get caught up in the jazz culture of the 1920s. Instead of visiting speakeasies, Frank and Morrow Graham were busy building a new home for their growing family. In 1924 Billy's brother, Melvin, was born. Three years later, the Grahams moved from the small wooden house with

The Graham Brothers Dairy in about 1930

outdoor bathrooms to a two-story brick house with indoor plumbing. Billy and Melvin shared a bedroom and grew to be very close, despite the six-year age difference between them.

The Roaring Twenties came to a sudden halt in 1929, when the stock market crashed. Banks and businesses closed, causing millions of people to lose all of their money. Billy's father lost his life savings—four thousand dollars—when his local bank failed following the 1929 stock market crash. Yet the dairy farm always had some customers. Milk was one of the staples for which people spent their last bit of money, even during extremely hard times. In the early 1930s, when milk prices fell to five cents a quart, the Graham Brothers Dairy almost went bankrupt. But Frank and Clyde managed to hold on through those difficult years. Extreme poverty spread across the entire United States, with thousands of people out of work and jobs almost impossible to find. That period (1929–1942) is called the Great Depression.

LIFE ON THE FARM

A dairy farm, where children saw all stages of life and death, was an interesting place to grow up. Billy, Catherine, and Melvin had plenty of pet dogs, cats, and even goats. Billy and Catherine sometimes hooked a cart to one of their goats and had the goat pull them around the farm while they pretended to be helping their father. On rainy days, Billy would often sneak into the barn, where he enjoyed listening for hours to the tapping of raindrops on the tin roof. His mother taught him to read before he started school, and he plowed through books, from the Bible to the Hardy Boys adventure series. Occasionally, on Saturday evenings, the whole family would pile into the car and head for the country grocery store—or sometimes as far as Niven's Drugstore in Charlotte—for a treat. Billy's father bought each child an ice-cream cone or a soda, and they would enjoy them in the car while Frank went to the barbershop for a shave.

Until he started school, Billy spent almost all his time with his family, so he felt nervous on his first day at elementary school. His mother packed him a lunch and told him that he could eat it during recess. When the teacher announced a ten-minute recess at ten in the morning, Billy quickly wolfed down the contents of his lunch box. He didn't realize that the lunchtime recess was at noon. While the other children slowly enjoyed their lunches at noon, Billy had nothing to eat. By the time school ended at three in the afternoon, he was starving. He raced out the door, eager to get home and eat something. But the principal thought he was being disrespectful and yanked him back into school by his ear.

As soon as they were old enough to help, all the Graham children were responsible for real chores. For most of his early life, Billy got out of bed at 2:30 in the morning to help milk cows. Feeling as though he had fallen asleep just a few minutes earlier, Billy climbed out of his warm bed and ran down the lane to wake the farmworkers. One worker, Pedro, called the cows to come into the milking house, and then everyone got to work. Carrying his three-legged stool, Billy moved in and out of twenty stalls. He fastened restraining chains on the cows' hind legs to keep from getting kicked and milked all twenty cows in about two hours. The job was hard work, resulting in sore hands from milking and an occasional bruised face from a swift swish of a cow's tail. But Billy did not complain. He knew it was part of his responsibility as a family member, and he was happy he could help out.

The Graham family's religion helped them remain optimistic throughout the Great Depression. They had faith that God would protect them when they really needed help, and they were not afraid of the future. In 1932 Billy's sister Jean was born. Just a few weeks later, Frank Graham suffered an almost fatal accident. The farm's manager was using an electric saw to chop wood. As Frank approached him with a question, the saw caught a log and sent a chunk of wood flying into Frank's mouth, smashing his jaw and almost cutting off his head. He nearly bled to death as he was rushed to the hospital. Most people didn't expect him to recover, but his wife and friends prayed for him. When he did make a full recovery, he thought that God must have been protecting him in answer to prayers. His faith in God was greatly strengthened by the experience.

RESISTING RELIGION

By the time Billy was in high school, both his parents were becoming more serious about their religion. After his accident, Billy's father invited a group of Christian businessmen from Charlotte to hold their all-day prayer meetings on his farm. Billy's mother often entertained and prayed with the members' wives during these events. On her own, she also read the Bible's New Testament over and over, paying particular attention to the Book of Revelation, which describes the second coming, or return, of Jesus

*Baptist evangelist
Dr. Mordecai Fowler
Ham is shown here in
an advertisement from
1935. Billy heard him
preach in 1934.*

REV. M. F. HAM
LOUISVILLE, KY.
Evangelist, Bible Teacher and Lecturer.

Christ. She also read books and articles by famous Bible teachers and evangelists.

Meanwhile, in 1934, when Billy was fifteen, a famous and controversial evangelist named Dr. Mordecai Fowler Ham came to Charlotte for a three-month stay. During this stay, he preached almost every night of the week at a makeshift church built to seat five thousand people on the outskirts of Charlotte. Ham was famous for his energetic commitment to the Gospel and his passionate preaching. He was controversial because some people thought he was anti-Semitic—biased against Jewish people. Billy's parents went to hear Ham talk and were impressed by his powerful discussions of the Gospel. As an evangelist, he focused on saving people's souls by convincing them to commit their lives to God. Billy's father said, "My experience is that Ham's meetings opened my eyes to the truth." His mother agreed.

But at fifteen, Billy did not share his parents' enthusiasm for the Gospel. He was more interested in playing baseball and driving his father's car as fast as he could. For his whole life, he had accompanied his parents to church and participated in family Bible readings. However, he did these things more out of a sense of duty than out of a passion for God. He would have called himself a Christian, but he felt he did not quite know what that meant. When his parents asked him to come along to hear Ham preach, he said no. Then, a few weeks later, a friend—who was already a committed Christian—convinced him to go hear Ham. Actually, Billy agreed to go mostly so he could drive his friend's truck. Once he got there, however, he was won over by Ham. After his first visit, he returned night after night. The fiery preacher talked about God's love. He also warned the audience that they were headed for hell if they did not save their souls by committing their lives to God.

COMMITTED TO JESUS

Ham's sermons were meant to frighten people so they would mend their ways. Billy found himself increasingly attracted to the idea of committing himself to a life with Jesus Christ. He realized that he had never really thought about himself as a Christian outside of his family. But suddenly he began to see that he needed to commit to being the best Christian he could be. He began to realize that being saved and being "right with God" was important to him.

It is common for evangelical preachers to give "invitations" to their audience. They invite people to come to the front of the church and publicly accept Jesus Christ into their lives. Although Billy had been baptized as a baby, he realized that as a young adult, he needed to accept Christ on his own—with purpose and intention. One evening he accepted Ham's invitation and walked to the front of the church. He later recalled that he walked "as if I had lead weights attached to my feet." Nearly four hundred other people stood with Billy near the church platform that night, publicly committing themselves to Christ. Billy's father came up and put his arm around Billy's shoulder, telling Billy how thankful he was to see him commit himself.

Billy had no doubts about his new commitment to Christ, but he did worry about what his friends and teachers would say. At school some people teased him, and a few began calling him "preacher." But Billy found the change within himself was so strong that he did not mind the teasing. He also reminded himself that Ham had warned that Christians often face harassment for their beliefs. Billy went to hear Ham

Seventeen-year-old Billy grins for this 1935 photo. He was a lively teenager.

during his entire stay in Charlotte. After Ham left, Billy wanted to go to his own church as often as he could, and he looked forward to it all week. He also joined in other church activities.

Billy felt that his life had changed dramatically, but apart from going to church more often, his routine remained the same for his last two years of high school. He did his chores on the farm, went to school, played baseball and went to ball games with his friends. He often found it hard to concentrate at school after rising so early each morning to milk cows, and his grades began to suffer. After earning As through elementary school, his grades slipped to mostly Cs in high school. In tenth grade, he failed French and had to make it up in summer school.

During summer break, Billy also delivered Graham Brothers Dairy milk to customers in Charlotte. He went to see any evangelists that came through Charlotte to preach. Many of these traveling preachers were invited to stay at the Graham family home while they were in town. Two of these men, Jimmie Johnson and Fred Brown, were graduates of the Bob Jones College in Cleveland, Tennessee. They convinced Billy and his parents that this would be the perfect college for Billy.

In May 1936, Billy graduated with twenty-five other seniors from Sharon High School. He planned to attend Bob Jones College in the fall. But first, he had a plan with his friend Albert McMakin to earn some money for school. Albert had gotten a job with the Fuller Brush Company selling high-quality cleaning brushes across the southern states. Billy convinced his father—who did not want to lose a good milker and delivery driver—to let him accept a job with Fuller as a traveling salesman. So Billy, Albert, and two other high school friends set out across South Carolina. They stopped at every small town they drove through and spent their days walking door-to-door, convincing people to buy their brushes. At night they slept in boardinghouses for one dollar a night—sometimes sharing their beds with bedbugs. Some weeks Billy earned up to seventy-five dollars, which was quite a lot of money in the 1930s. It would help pay his expenses at Bob Jones College in the fall.

Graham (center) *did not last long at Bob Jones College. He moved on to the Florida Bible Institute after just a few months. Its dean, Dr. John Minder* (left), *arranged for Graham to give his first sermon.*

Chapter **TWO**

A PREACHER'S CALLING

IN SEPTEMBER **1936,** BILLY GRAHAM HEADED WEST to Bob Jones College. His father drove him across the Appalachian Mountains to Cleveland, Tennessee. Billy was eager to get to work at his new school and to deepen his understanding of God and Christianity. A sign in his dormitory room, Griping Not Tolerated, greeted him.

Billy was prepared for hard work, and he had no plans to gripe. But from his first days at Bob Jones College, he felt the school was not right for him. Although his parents had been strict with him when he was growing up, he was not prepared for the stern rules of Bob Jones College. Dating was very restricted. All dates between young men and young women had to be approved and scheduled. At other times, male students and female students were not allowed to talk to one another. Billy was surprised by these rules, but he knew he could live with them. Still, something did not seem quite right. While he liked Dr. Bob Jones, he was not sure he agreed with the way he taught the Bible. "I disliked being told what to think without being given the opportunity to reason issues through on my own or to look at other viewpoints," he later recalled. Billy grew even more uncomfortable toward the end of the semester, when he met with Dr. Jones to tell him about his worries. Instead of understanding, Dr. Jones screamed at Billy and told him he was a failure.

Several of Billy's friends were also unhappy at Bob Jones. One of his roommates left the school and entered the Florida Bible Institute in Temple Terrace, Florida, about fifteen miles east of Tampa. The Graham family had already planned a winter vacation to Florida, so Billy visited the school. He immediately felt comfortable there. He returned to Bob Jones in January for the second semester, but within a month, he was accepted at the Florida Bible Institute. He moved there in late January.

HOME IN FLORIDA

After the cold, rainy winter weather in Cleveland, the new school in Florida felt like a resort. In fact, the institute was housed in a former hotel with pink stucco buildings, wrought iron railings, and a golf course. The rest of the town of Temple Terrace was practically deserted. It had been planned as an exclusive community in the 1920s, but only a few houses had been finished before the stock market crash of 1929. The school's seventy students—forty women and thirty men—lived at the hotel. Visitors rented the other rooms for a few days or even months. The students worked in the kitchen, cooking, serving meals, and cleaning up.

Billy immediately felt as though he had found a new family. He took classes in Bible study, church history, and theology—the general study of religion. A big part of the school's mission was to teach students how to spread the Bible's message. Students regularly preached in local churches, trailer parks, street corners, and even jails. Billy grew more and more comfortable speaking in public. The school encouraged students to think for themselves and to ask questions—exactly the opposite of Bob Jones. In a letter home, Billy told his mother how happy he was at his new school: "Mother, words can't express Florida Bible Institute. . . . I love it here."

During Easter break, the institute's dean, Dr. John Minder, invited Billy to visit his family property and conference center in northern Florida. While there, a local Baptist preacher asked Minder to fill in for him at his church. Instead, Minder offered to have Billy preach. Billy was shocked, excited, and scared all at once, but he couldn't turn down his dean. Luckily, Billy had been working for months on four sermons. He had polished them and practiced them in front of a mirror, but he had never actually delivered one to a live audience. He spent the next two days repeating them over and over, studying, and worrying about how he would perform.

On the morning of the service, he arrived at the church to find about forty people waiting. He remembered later that "when the moment came to walk to the pulpit . . . my knees shook and my perspiration glistened on my hands." He began with his first and favorite sermon. But it seemed like it was over almost immediately. The audience looked at him expectantly. So he launched into his second sermon. Before he knew it, he had finished all four of his prepared sermons, and he took his seat again. When he looked at his watch, he realized it had taken him exactly eight minutes to deliver all four sermons. People later described his early preaching style as similar to machine-gun fire.

Billy returned to school after his first preaching experience determined to improve his skills. He began composing more and more sermons, using outlines he found in his textbooks. He paddled a canoe to a small, nearby island and practiced his delivery to the trees, alligators, and birds living there. Sometimes he returned to find a group of students teasing and applauding him on his expert preaching.

FINDING NEW FAITH

Despite the teasing, Billy was becoming more and more certain that God was calling him to be a preacher. For years he had known that he would dedicate his life to serving God, but he had not been sure what form his service would take. He didn't think he had the talent or the desire to preach full-time. But over the next year, he began preaching to Sunday night youth groups at Minder's church, the Tampa Gospel Tabernacle. Soon Minder was inviting Billy to fill in for him at his regular Sunday services. Then other preachers asked him to fill in at their churches. Billy became more and more certain of his skills as a preacher.

While a student at the Florida Bible Institute in the 1930s, Graham briefly served as an associate pastor at Alliance Church in Tampa.

But Billy found that his favorite experiences were not preaching in church. They were preaching to residents of local trailer parks. He began to preach every Sunday at the Tin Can Trailer Park near Tampa. He had audiences that ranged from two hundred to one thousand people. During these events, Billy tried to convince as many residents as possible to convert to Christianity and commit their lives to Christ. His success at this convinced him that this was his true calling, but he remained unsure if he had the drive to preach for the rest of his life. One night he prayed and told God that if he wanted him to serve as a preacher, he would. Later, Billy recalled that he received no specific sign from God. Yet he was certain from that night on that he was called by God to be a preacher.

In the summer of 1938, Minder asked Billy to return for a week of sermons to the northern Florida Baptist church where he had made his debut a year earlier. While he was there, he also filled in on a daily Gospel radio show. During that week, Billy decided to be rebaptized as an adult. He had been baptized as an infant when water was sprinkled on his head at his parents' Presbyterian church. Years later, as a schoolboy, he had been confirmed in a Presbyterian church, when he declared his personal allegiance to God. Billy knew he was committed to his faith. But he wanted to be baptized as a Baptist, since he was preaching in a Baptist church. According to Baptist custom, a person should be fully immersed in water to signify rebirth as a committed Christian. So Billy asked a preacher friend to baptize him. Billy waded into the small lake next to the church. The preacher lowered him quickly under water for less than three seconds total. When Billy waded ashore again, he was a baptized Baptist.

"YOUNG MAN WITH A BURNING MESSAGE"

From his earliest years, Billy Graham was a master of self-promotion. When he began preaching in Florida in the late 1930s, he often had trouble engaging his audience. But he had no trouble improving his appeal. In self-written brochures, he described himself as a "Young Man with a Burning Message," or a "Dynamic Youthful Evangelist." Soon he was plastering the small Florida towns in which he was preaching with posters and brochures: "Great Gospel Preacher" and "One of America's Outstanding Young Evangelists."

Once he mailed his friend Grady Wilson one of his brochures for First Baptist Church of Capitola. On it he had scribbled, "Big Baptist church in the capital of Florida. Pray for me." Grady impulsively drove all the way to the revival. Billy was stunned to see Grady strolling down Capitola's one dusty street. Billy suspected he was in trouble because Grady was a relentless needler. He had brought high-flying Billy down to earth many times.

"Capitola is just a tiny logging town, buddy," observed Grady, grinning.

Billy laughed. "That's not all. The revival got canceled. The local pastor had to leave unexpectedly. Do you need a thousand brochures?"

The next logical step for Billy was to become an ordained Baptist minister. This meant that he would be set apart for the duty of preaching the Gospel. It also allowed him to perform weddings, funerals, and other official church business. Billy later described ordination as being designated as God's servant to other people. Billy had the academic background to be ordained. He also had plenty of preaching experience. To make it official, a council of five Baptist pastors was formed. One Sunday, Billy sat down across a table from them and answered their questions about his background and his beliefs. After the council approved him for ordination, a service was set for that evening. Billy knelt on a small platform at the front of the church. The five pastors stood around him and lightly touched their fingertips to his head as they prayed for him. When he stood up, he was an ordained Baptist minister. In many religions, pastors have to graduate from seminary—a school that trains people to become ministers, priests, or rabbis. But this ritual was the only requirement to become an ordained Baptist minister.

Up North

During Billy's senior year at the Florida Bible Institute, he became friends with a guest from Chicago who was staying at the school's hotel. This guest's brother was the chairman of the board of Wheaton College, a private Christian college near Chicago.

Billy's new friend convinced him that Wheaton would be an excellent place for Billy to complete his studies once he graduated from the Florida Bible Institute. After graduation in May 1940, Billy and a classmate headed north. They stopped first in York, Pennsylvania, where Billy had been invited to preach for a week. He was so popular during that week that he was asked to stay an extra week. After that, the friends headed to New York City for a day at the World's Fair. There, Billy saw his first television.

Next, Billy spent a month in North Carolina with his family, and then he headed for Wheaton College in September 1940. Wheaton was a strict Christian liberal arts school. All students were required to study the Bible for four years. Dancing, card playing, smoking, and drinking alcohol were forbidden. Since the Florida Bible Institute had been a small religious school, Wheaton did not give Billy credit for all of the classes he had taken there. Billy entered Wheaton as a second-semester freshman. For the first time in his life, his fellow students would include African Americans. At this time, black students and white students went to segregated, or separate, schools in the South.

From the start, Billy stood out from most Wheaton students. At twenty-one, he was three years older than most of the other freshmen. At six feet two inches tall, he was also taller than most of them and had an unmistakable southern drawl. Although he felt out of place and homesick at times, he was busy with his studies and he made friends. Instead of concentrating on Bible studies, as he had done at the Florida Bible Institute, he chose to major in anthropology (the study of the customs and development of human beings). He felt that his career as a preacher might take him on missions to foreign countries. The study of other cultures would help him.

In 1941 the United States entered World War II (1939–1945). Billy considered joining the army and being a chaplain. As a chaplain, he would lead religious services and counsel people in the army. Billy thought it would be a way to serve his country and God at the same time. But in order to become a chaplain, he would first need to graduate from Wheaton and then take a course at a seminary.

At Wheaton, Billy studied hard to do well in classes such as anthropology, Greek, and economics. But he also found time to fall in love with a fellow student, Ruth Bell. Ruth was the daughter of missionaries— representatives of a church who travel to foreign countries to teach their religion. She had grown up in China. Ruth was as committed to Christianity as Billy was, and she hoped to become a missionary herself when she graduated. She wouldn't go out on dates on Saturday nights, saying she spent that time prayerfully preparing for Sunday. During Billy's first months at Wheaton, the two grew closer and closer, and Billy tried to convince Ruth to marry him. But Ruth was concerned that marrying would keep her from her true calling of being a missionary. In the spring semester, she had to leave school abruptly to care for her ill sister. Ruth and Billy had not yet settled on marriage. But that summer, while Billy was at home in North Carolina, he received a letter from Ruth. She wrote that she would marry him. Billy was overjoyed.

Graham married Ruth Bell in 1943.

Chapter **THREE**

FROM PASTOR
TO EVANGELIST

BILLY GRAHAM AND RUTH BELL BOTH GRADUATED from Wheaton College in June 1943. Two months later, they were married at Ruth's parents' house in Montreat, North Carolina. The Grahams spent their honeymoon in the nearby Blue Ridge Mountains before driving back to Chicago. Graham had been offered a job as a pastor at Western Springs Baptist Church, about twenty miles southeast of Wheaton College. A church member found a furnished apartment for the young couple.

RADIO PREACHER

After busy years in college and planning for their wedding, the Grahams enjoyed the quiet routine of life in the small town of Hinsdale, Illinois. Western Springs was a small church with about one hundred members. Only about fifty of those members regularly went to church on Sundays. During the week, Graham studied and wrote his sermons. Ruth helped him find real-life examples to illustrate the Bible readings he chose. Graham's sermons were popular. Soon almost one hundred people were coming to church every Sunday. Graham also changed the name of the church from Western Springs Baptist Church to Village Church, since there were few Baptists in the area but many members of other Christian religions.

Since their apartment was furnished, the Grahams didn't need to do much to their home. They liked not having to buy a lot of furniture and other items. Graham still planned on becoming an army chaplain as soon as he could qualify. For the time being, he was busy with his duties as a pastor. He preached twice on Sundays and then attended youth Bible groups at members' homes. During the week, he held a prayer meeting, and both Grahams taught children's Bible classes.

Graham did not have much extra time. But one day, he received an offer he could not refuse. Torrey Johnson, a pastor who had two popular preaching programs on the radio, offered to let Graham take over one of them. The program was called *Songs in the Night*. It was a live Sunday night program that mixed music with preaching. It would cost Graham's church

$150 a week to pay the Chicago radio station for the airtime. But it would be heard throughout the midwestern states and even in some southern and eastern states.

At first the church governing board voted against doing the radio program, because it would be too expensive. But soon a wealthy church member offered to pay the fees, and Graham was set to do the program. Then Graham's excitement turned to worry. How would he ever get a big enough audience to listen to him, an unknown preacher from a tiny Illinois church? Graham quickly solved the problem by convincing a well-known religious radio personality, George Beverly Shea, also called Bev Shea, to sing on the program. The show was broadcast live on Sunday evenings from the basement of the Village Church. People across the Midwest heard about the church and started coming to the Sunday night services. When the *Chicago Tribune* newspaper reported on Graham's show, people from across the country sent in money to support it. Billy Graham was becoming famous. Churches around the Midwest started asking him to come and preach.

Preaching to Youth

Soon after the radio program began to take off, Graham was accepted into the U.S. Army chaplain program. He would take a course at the Divinity School of Harvard University in Cambridge, Massachusetts, and then become a chaplain. It was exactly what he had been waiting for, but his health got in the way. He came down with a severe case of mumps, an acute virus marked by fever and swelling glands. Graham had to spend several weeks in bed. He missed the Harvard course. Although he was officially a member of the U.S. Army, he would have to wait to be a chaplain until he could take the seminary class.

Once the worst of Graham's illness was over, he and Ruth decided to take a short trip to Florida to complete his recovery. While in Florida, they discovered that Pastor Torrey Johnson was vacationing nearby. Johnson had been impressed by Graham's radio show, and he had another offer for him. He wanted Graham to become a full-time evangelist for a new group he was forming, Youth for Christ (YFC) International. This group aimed to provide evangelistic meetings—with music and prayer—for young people and the armed forces. Johnson wanted Graham to be the group's first full-time employee. Graham would help organize and preach at youth rallies in the United States, Canada, and, eventually, the rest of the world.

Graham was excited by the idea, but he had two other obligations: to Village Church and to the U.S. Army. Nevertheless, Johnson convinced Graham that traveling and preaching the Gospel to young people was the perfect job for him. In December 1944, Village Church accepted Graham's resignation. The U.S. Army granted him a discharge since it looked pretty

Graham was a dynamic preacher from the start. He is shown here speaking in Grand Rapids, Michigan, in the 1940s.

certain that the war was ending soon. Graham became a Youth for Christ evangelist. In his new job, he traveled across the country, organizing rallies for young Christians. The YFC rallies included lively Gospel music, personal stories of coming to God, and short sermons. He enjoyed the job, but he missed Ruth while he was traveling. Then in the spring of 1945, Ruth discovered she was pregnant. The couple decided that Ruth should not spend so much time alone in Illinois. They moved in with Ruth's parents, and Graham continued to travel. The Grahams' first daughter, Virginia (Gigi) Leftwich Graham, was born September 21, 1945, while Graham was away on a trip.

Soon Graham was traveling even farther away from home. In 1946 he took his first trip abroad. He spent March and April preaching at YFC rallies in England, Scotland, Ireland, Sweden, Holland, Denmark, Belgium, and France. He teamed up with a singer, Cliff Barrows. Thousands of young Americans and Europeans attended the meetings. Having lived through a devastating war, many people welcomed the message of hope in God that the evangelists preached. At the end of each evening, Graham invited people to come forward and commit themselves to Christ. Night after night, many young people made this commitment. The tour was very successful. As soon as they arrived home in the United States, the YFC team—Graham, singer Cliff Barrows, and Barrows's wife Billie, who played the piano—planned a return trip to Great Britain and France.

The Grahams didn't like being apart from each other for such long periods. They decided to travel together and leave one-year-old Gigi with Ruth's parents. Ruth led prayers during the rallies. The Grahams were glad to spend some time together, but a trip to Europe in the mid-1940s was not exactly a vacation. The war had spread destruction and caused shortages of many staples such as eggs, milk, and fuel to heat buildings. The YFC team often slept in damp, cold rooms and ate powdered eggs for breakfast. But thousands of young people turned out at rallies each night, and the trip was a big success.

YOUNG COLLEGE PRESIDENT

Back in the United States, Graham met many famous religious leaders while traveling for Youth for Christ. One of these was the evangelist and educator Dr. W. B. Riley. Riley was the president of Northwestern Schools, a Bible school, liberal arts college, and seminary in Minneapolis, Minnesota. In the summer of 1947, after

The main building on the Northwestern Schools campus in Minneapolis, Minnesota, in 1967. Graham accepted a job as president at the college.

Graham spoke at a conference near Minneapolis, Riley asked that Graham visit him at his home. When Graham arrived, he found the eighty-six-year-old man very ill. Riley surprised Graham by asking him to take over as president of Northwestern Schools.

At first Graham didn't know what to say. He felt that God had called him to spread the word of the Bible through preaching. He was already building a career with Youth for Christ. Also, he didn't feel qualified to be a college president. He didn't have an advanced degree—a master's or a doctorate—like most college presidents. But he felt that being an educator could help him spread God's word, and Riley was sure that Graham was the right man for the job. Graham agreed to become vice president and to act as interim (temporary) president if anything happened to Riley.

Still, Graham was unprepared when Riley died in December 1947. The Northwestern Schools governing board voted Graham in as interim president. Billy Graham became the youngest college president in the country. Not everyone at the school liked having such a young, inexperienced preacher as president. But they knew that it was Riley's wish. Since Graham was still working full-time for Youth for Christ, he did not accept any salary for his job as president. He also knew that his family was happy living in North Carolina. They did not want to move to Minneapolis. Graham hired an old friend, T. W. Wilson, to be his vice president.

Graham worked closely with Bev Shea (left) *and Cliff Barrows* (right) *on Youth for Christ rallies around the United States.*

FINDING FAME

Throughout 1947 Graham became more and more famous as the face of Youth for Christ. Bev Shea had joined Graham's team. Together with Shea and Cliff Barrows, Graham led hundreds of rallies across the United States that year. He reached thousands of young people. Soon churches and other Christian groups began inviting the team to lead rallies that targeted not just young people but whole cities. By 1948 Graham began to concentrate more on these citywide meetings, called campaigns.

A campaign usually came about because a group of Christians in one city would ask Graham to lead meetings in a public space for several nights in a row. The campaign's sponsoring group raised money to pay for the rallies and to pay expenses for Graham and his team. Although there were no ticket fees, people who attended the rallies would usually donate money at the end of the night. The money was used to pay back the sponsoring group. Once enough money was raised to cover expenses, a "love offering" was collected—usually on the last evening of the campaign—for Graham and Barrows. (Bev Shea earned a wage for each meeting, but Graham and Barrows were paid only from these offerings at the end of a campaign.) During 1948 Graham held citywide campaigns in Augusta, Georgia, and Modesto, California. He also continued to lead many Youth for Christ rallies around both the United States and Canada.

That year Graham received two honorary degrees. These degrees are given to honor people, without requiring them to complete the regular courses and exams. From King's College in Newcastle, Delaware, he received an honorary Doctorate of Divinity. From the school where he had first attended college, Bob Jones University, he received an honorary Doctorate of Humanities.

In September 1949, Graham went to Los Angeles to begin a citywide campaign. The campaign was scheduled to last three weeks. Graham hoped that it would be one of his most popular engagements ever. A huge tent was put up in downtown Los Angeles for the nightly events. Graham even held his first press conference a few days before the campaign was scheduled to begin. A handful of reporters showed up at the press conference to ask Graham questions about the campaign. But the next day, not one newspaper carried a story about it. Graham was beginning to worry that he wouldn't attract very big crowds in Los Angeles. And on the first few nights, only about three thousand people showed up. This was a large crowd, but not large enough to fill the huge tent. But each night, Graham's preaching grew more and more fiery, urging people to turn away from sin and toward God's love. His message was that God created and loves the human race, even though people turn their backs on him. Graham stood on a large platform in front of a twenty-foot tall replica of a Bible. Each night many people accepted Graham's invitation to commit themselves to Christ. Soon word was spreading around the city.

The Los Angeles campaign was scheduled to end on October 16. But as that date approached, it was obvious that the people's excitement about the campaign was picking up. Graham and his team decided to extend the campaign. Each night larger crowds showed up to hear Billy Graham preach.

One evening dozens of newspaper reporters showed up. The next day, the *Los Angeles Examiner* had a morning headline about the campaign. The evening paper, the *Los Angeles Herald Express,* also carried a front-page story.

Newspaper headlines helped Graham meet the challenge to fill the enormous tent erected for the 1949 Los Angeles campaign.

"KISSED BY WILLIAM RANDOLPH HEARST"

Much of the success of Billy Graham's 1949 Los Angeles campaign can be traced to the extensive newspaper coverage it received. And this media attention can be traced to one man: William Randolph Hearst. Hearst was the publisher of the morning *Los Angeles Examiner*, the evening *Los Angeles Herald Express*, and more than twenty-five other national newspapers. In the 1940s, Hearst had the power to create news that convinced others to follow his beliefs. One of his beliefs was that Communism was evil. Communism is a totalitarian system of government in which the state controls the economy. Communist countries usually prohibit the practice of religion. Hearst recognized strong anti-

William Randolph Hearst

Communist feelings in Graham's preaching so he decided to publicize the relatively unknown preacher during his Los Angeles campaign.

In his autobiography, Graham recalled that his nightly appearances in Los Angeles were receiving very little press coverage. Then, one night, Graham arrived to find dozens of reporters and camera people filling the tent. When he asked one of the journalists why they were all there, the reporter replied, "You've just been kissed by William Randolph Hearst." Indeed, the next day, both of Hearst's Los Angeles papers carried feature stories about the campaign. Papers across the country soon picked up the story. Later, some of Hearst's top editors recalled that they had been instructed to write positively about Graham. The publicity helped launch Billy Graham as a national figure.

Graham preaches with dramatic gestures as his fame continues to grow in the late 1940s and early 1950s.

Soon newspapers around the country were printing stories about Billy Graham and the Los Angeles campaign. In November *Time* magazine carried the story. The *Time* reporter described Graham's preaching style: "Blond, trumpet-lunged North Carolinian William Franklin Graham, Jr., a Southern Baptist minister who is also president of the Northwestern Schools in Minneapolis, dominates his huge audience from the moment he strides onstage to the strains of 'Send the Great Revival in My Soul.' His lapel microphone, which gives added volume to his deep voice, allows him to pace the platform as he walks, rising to his toes to drive home a point, clenching his fists, stabbing his finger at the sky and straining to get his words to the furthermost corners of the tent." By the time the Los Angeles campaign finally ended, on November 20, hundreds of thousands of people had heard Graham preach. Thousands had accepted Christ for the first time or recommitted themselves to making him part of their daily lives. And Billy Graham, a farm boy from North Carolina, had become famous across the United States.

Billy Graham had already become a celebrity by 1950.

Chapter **FOUR**

SPREADING THE WORD

BY **1950** MOST AMERICANS KNEW WHO BILLY Graham was. This popularity helped him to do the work he believed God wanted him to do—to lead people to Christ and help them commit their daily lives to him. His theme remained the same. He always preached the message of "God's redemptive love for sinners and the need for personal redemption and conversion." But the popularity also made Graham's life more complicated. Suddenly thousands of people were sending him money to continue his work. He needed to make sure that the money was handled honestly and that people knew they could trust him to use it for his work. To make this easier, he founded the Billy Graham Evangelistic Association (BGEA).

The association would handle the growing business of Graham and his team. The BGEA rented an office across the street from Northwestern Schools in Minneapolis. Graham began to receive a set salary instead of love offerings.

As one of its first official acts, the association changed the name of its citywide meetings from *campaigns* to *crusades*. Evangelists had been leading campaigns for many years. Many Americans were familiar with the term. Unfortunately, the word was often associated with attention-hungry preachers who were unscrupulous about money and often used their supporters to make themselves rich. Graham and his team wanted to make it clear that they followed a new kind of evangelism, and they felt the word *crusade* best described their mission of bringing people to Christ.

RADIO AND MOVIES

From the beginning, the Billy Graham Evangelistic Association had plenty of work. Graham and his team were finding new ways to reach people. They knew that getting the Bible's message out to the largest number of people was the key to getting people to commit their lives to Christ. So they turned to technology to help them reach mass audiences. In 1950 most American houses still did not have television. But many Americans did have access to radio and movies.

Graham already had experience in radio preaching from his *Songs in the Night* show almost ten years earlier. By 1950 radio evangelists were being heard across the country. One of the most well-known radio preachers was Dr. Walter Maier. When Maier died in 1950, Graham prayed that another persuasive radio personality would come along to take his place. Other people were praying for the same thing. Many of them thought Billy Graham would be the best person for the job. For weeks two broadcasting agents tried to convince Graham to take Maier's place on a weekly radio broadcast. But Graham knew he was far too busy to take on radio preaching. He was still president of Northwestern Schools, he was leading huge citywide crusades, and he was still working for Youth for Christ.

The two radio agents followed Graham across the country, from preaching events in Michigan to Oregon. At first Graham appreciated their eagerness. But after he told them many times that he was not ready to take on a radio show, he began to be annoyed that they would not leave him alone. Finally, one evening in Portland, Oregon, the men told Graham that they were giving up. They were leaving for the airport to go home. Graham was glad to hear this. He joked, "All right fellows, if before midnight tonight I should get twenty-five thousand dollars for the purpose of a radio broadcast, I'll take that as an answer to prayer and be willing to do a national broadcast."

The radio men laughed at this. That evening a crowd of seventeen thousand at a Greater Portland Gospel crusade also laughed when Graham told the story. But after the meeting ended, thousands of people stayed to offer donations to help with the radio broadcast. By the time Graham headed back to his hotel, he had received twenty-four thousand dollars. Graham didn't know whether to take it as a sign that God wanted him to do the radio broadcast or not. It seemed like a sign, but the fund was one thousand dollars short. Unbelievably, when Graham arrived at his hotel, he found two letters from supporters, each with a check for five hundred dollars. So he knew for certain that God wanted him to preach on the radio, and he called the two radio agents. On November 5, 1950, the first of the new weekly *Hour of Decision* programs was broadcast from Atlanta, Georgia. One month later, Graham's third daughter, Ruth Bell Graham, was born. Family and friends called her Bunny when she was an infant, and the name stuck.

Meanwhile, the Portland crusade had also been the subject of the first-ever Billy Graham film. Great Commission Films made a color documentary movie of the Portland crusade. It had lasted for six weeks and attracted more than half a million people. This film was shown in churches throughout the northwestern United States. But Graham decided that even more people might come to see a fictional movie about a crusade. He decided to make such a movie

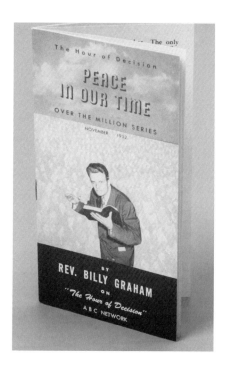

A November 1952 publication advertises Graham's weekly radio broadcast, The Hour of Decision.

during his next citywide campaign, scheduled for Fort Worth, Texas, in February and March of 1951. A story was written about a rodeo rider who comes to the crusade and decides to commit his life to Christ. The movie, *Mr. Texas*, was the first Billy Graham feature film. Graham rented the Hollywood Bowl, a huge outdoor stadium in Hollywood, California, to show the film for the first time. One night in early October 1951, searchlights crisscrossed the Hollywood sky as more than thirty thousand watched the premiere of *Mr. Texas*.

Across the Ocean

Graham's family continued to grow. His son William Franklin Graham III was born on July 14, 1952. Graham continued to attract huge audiences in citywide crusades across the United States. In 1952 more than 300,000 people turned out for the Washington, D.C., crusade. More than 450,000 came to see Graham in Houston, Texas, and he spoke to more than 360,000 during his Jackson, Mississippi, crusade. He even went overseas to preach to U.S. troops stationed in Korea and Japan. That year he resigned as president of Northwestern Schools so he could concentrate on preaching.

With all his success in the United States, Graham began to think about spreading the word of Christ around the world. Even though Graham had preached in Europe, Korea, and Japan, he had spoken mostly to U.S. audiences. He had never held a full-scale citywide crusade in another country. But in 1952, he began planning to hold one in London. He even visited Great Britain that year to meet with some businesspeople who wanted to sponsor the crusade. Church leaders in Great Britain were interested to hear from Graham about his success in the United States. He spoke to a large group of British clergy in 1952. The group was impressed by Graham's excitement about the potential of citywide crusades to lead people to Christ. They were also impressed by his honesty. He talked about three main dangers of his kind of large-scale evangelism. Those dangers were getting people carried away with false emotions, convincing people to commit to Christ and having them soon change their minds, and becoming too preoccupied with money. Graham talked about how hard the BGEA worked to prevent these dangers.

Back in the United States, Graham met with several important British businesspeople and church leaders. This group made a commitment to sponsor a Billy Graham crusade in London in 1954. Graham laid out two conditions for his visit. He wanted the united support of British churches. He knew that without the support of the churches he would not be successful. He didn't want to compete with the churches. After all, Graham's goal was to increase long-term membership in the churches. He wanted to inspire people to be more active in whatever church they belonged to. His second condition was that a large sum of money be spent on advertising. He thought that in a city as huge as London, it would be impossible to draw a large crowd without massive advertising.

The details were worked out. In February 1954, Graham and his team boarded the SS *United States*, bound for Great Britain. Arriving at Southampton in southern England, the Grahams were mobbed by newspaper reporters and ordinary citizens. Many of the reporters demanded answers to rude questions such as "What are you doing here anyway?" and

"Don't you think you're more needed in your own country?" But the ordinary people gave the team a warm welcome. A customs worker shook Graham's hand and said, "Welcome to England and good luck, sir. We need you." Graham took the train to London and was again greeted by a mob of well-wishers, photographers, and reporters. All the major London newspapers carried headlines of Billy Graham's arrival.

Reporters and well-wishers greet Graham (in the center of the photo, to the right of the tipped hat) *at the London train station in 1954.*

Nightly meetings were scheduled at London's indoor twelve-thousand-seat Harringay Arena. Despite all the press attention, it looked like attendance for the first night would be disappointing. That afternoon it began to sleet. In his hotel room, Graham received a phone call from team members already at the arena. They had expected it to be half full by then, but only about two thousand people had shown up. Graham was afraid of becoming a laughingstock if only two thousand people attended. But he believed that whatever happened would be God's will. As he and Ruth were driven up to the arena's entrance, he saw no lines at the door. He resigned himself to an unsuccessful event. As soon as he climbed out of the car, however, he heard someone yelling that the arena was jammed full of people. The main entrance was on the other side from where the Grahams had driven up so they could not see the crowds. When they walked inside, the arena was indeed full. People were standing and singing hymns. Graham preached on the topic "Does God Matter?" At the end of the evening, when he invited people to come forward and accept Christ, more than two hundred people did.

As the London campaign continued, it grew more and more popular. On the first Saturday night, the arena was full more than an hour before Graham was even scheduled to arrive. When he did arrive, more than thirty thousand people were crowded outside the arena. Each night hundreds of people accepted Graham's invitation to join Christ. The meetings were so popular that all the major British newspapers interviewed Graham. Many of his sermons were carried on British radio. The Greater London crusade lasted three months and attracted more than two million people in all.

TO THE CORNERS OF THE WORLD

Graham and his team were exhausted by the end of the London crusade in May 1954. But they still planned to make a quick trip through Europe, holding one-day rallies in a dozen cities. After the publicity from the London crusade, however, the expected crowds would be too big for the theaters they had booked. On very short notice, they rebooked for the largest arenas they could find and planned to spend two days in some cities. Between June 16 and June 30, Graham preached to huge crowds—more than three hundred thousand—in Helsinki, Finland; Stockholm, Sweden; Amsterdam, Netherlands; the cities of Frankfurt, Dusseldorf, and Berlin in Germany; and Paris, France. In each city, interpreters translated Graham's sermon into the local language. Considering the language barriers, the turnout was impressive.

The huge success of the London crusade was a turning point in Graham's career. He knew that his message was meaningful outside the United States. At the end of 1954, the BGEA opened a permanent office in London. In March 1955, Graham and his team headed back to Europe for a six-week all-Scotland crusade,

A crowd carrying signs and banners welcomes Graham home from Europe in July 1954.

which drew more than three hundred thousand people. Immediately afterward, Graham and his team returned to London for another two-week crusade and an invitation to preach before Queen Elizabeth II. Another quick trip for rallies in France, Germany, and northern Europe reinforced the belief that Graham could reach people in many countries.

Soon Graham was thinking about a new challenge— the world beyond the United States and Europe. He felt strongly that the Christian faith had much to offer people all over the world, not just in countries where Christianity was already the main religion. So when the opportunity arose in 1955 to plan a trip to India, Graham was very excited. The trip was planned for early 1956. Graham would visit six Indian cities that already had small Christian churches. He knew that most of the people of India were quite poor, and he was eager to spread the Bible's message of hope. But he also knew that these would be very different crusades. Except for the small number of Christians, many Indians had never heard of the Bible. If they thought about Christianity at all, they may have thought it was a religion for white Europeans. The British had ruled India for many years before it became independent in 1947. Many Indians were not excited about the idea of sharing a religion with the West.

As Graham traveled through India, he preached the Gospel as he always did. He also delivered a special message about Jesus. He said, "I am not here to tell you about an American or a Britisher or a European. I am here to tell you about a man who was born right here in your part of the world, in Asia. He was born at the place where Asia and Africa and Europe meet. He had skin that was darker than mine and he came to show us all that God loves all people. He loves the people of India and he loves you." For four weeks, Graham held rallies across India, drawing huge crowds. Translators stood onstage with him and translated his message into several different Indian languages. Most

Indians are Hindu or Buddhist. Graham was careful not to attack the views of these or of any other religion. Instead, he tried to spread the word of Christ and especially to emphasize that Christianity is not a religion reserved for Europeans or white people. He hoped to convince many Asians of Christ's love. In New Delhi, Graham met with the Indian prime minister Jawaharlal Nehru, who was not a Christian but who wanted to welcome Graham and his team.

Arriving in Delhi, India, in February 1956, Graham (right) raises his hands in a traditional Hindu greeting to the crowd.

Before heading home to the United States, Graham traveled to other Asian countries including Taiwan, the Philippines, Japan, and Korea. Once home he began thinking about the large number of people in the world and how his travels were allowing him to reach more of them all the time. He also began thinking about other ways to reach people. *The Hour of Decision* was still being broadcast on the radio each week. (It had even had a brief run on television in 1954 to 1956.) The newly formed World Wide Pictures was still making documentary and feature films. But Graham thought that once a radio show or a movie is over, its impact stops. He believed that he could reach millions of people through a magazine, and in 1956, he helped launch *Christianity Today*. The magazine was written mostly for ministers. It aimed to reaffirm the power of the word of God to save men and women. Graham also saw the need for a magazine aimed at ordinary Christians. But he felt that the BGEA did not yet have the staff to produce one.

For the remainder of the 1950s, Graham continued to attract huge audiences to crusades in the United States and around the world. Almost two and a half million people attended the New York City crusade in the summer of 1957. Graham strongly believed in racial equality. He had always demanded that his audiences be integrated—that blacks be included and not separated from whites. Graham had torn down ropes put up to separate blacks and whites at a crusade in

Chattanooga, Tennessee. One night in New York, the civil rights leader Martin Luther King Jr. joined him onstage.

Graham found it challenging to balance his growing ministry with his growing family. The Graham's second son, Nelson Edman Graham (Ned), was born in May 1958. In 1960 he also realized his dream of publishing a magazine, *Decision*, to help ordinary Christians get closer to God. That year he attracted one million people during a tour of the Caribbean Islands. More than three million Australians and New Zealanders came to hear Graham when he toured those countries. He also visited the African countries of Liberia, Ghana, Nigeria, Rhodesia (later renamed Zimbabwe), Kenya, Ruanda (later renamed Rwanda), Ethiopia, and Egypt.

Sitting on the front step of the Graham home in Montreat, North Carolina, Graham's family poses for a photograph in 1960.
From left to right, *they are Franklin, Ruth (Bunny), Anne, Gigi, Ruth, and Ned.*

Chapter **FIVE**

STEPPING INTO POLITICS

BY 1960 BILLY GRAHAM HAD MET MANY world leaders. He had visited with President Harry Truman. He had attended the inauguration of President Dwight D. Eisenhower and remained friends with him throughout his two terms as president. Graham had also met with leaders from Europe, Asia, Africa, and South America. Despite these relationships and friendships with these leaders, Graham believed that he should stay out of politics. However, as he became familiar with political leaders, he found that he had to work at that.

PRESIDENTS KENNEDY AND JOHNSON

In 1960 Vice President Richard Nixon, a Republican, and Massachusetts senator John F. Kennedy, a Democrat, were running against each other for the U.S. presidency. Billy Graham knew and respected both men. People around the country were asking him to publicly support one of them. Graham did not want to do that.

Many Americans thought that Kennedy was not fit to be president because he was a Catholic. The Catholic Church recognizes the pope as its leader. Many people thought that it would be a conflict of interest for a U.S. president to support an international leader such as the pope. Also in those years,

Graham (left) *is seated next to John F. Kennedy at a prayer breakfast in the early 1960s.*

some Americans were prejudiced against Catholics in general, just as they were against people of different races and religions. Graham did not agree with this way of thinking. He wanted to state publicly that he would not vote against Kennedy because of his religion. But he was afraid that such a statement would be misunderstood as support for Kennedy. While Graham respected Kennedy, he was good friends with Nixon and planned to vote for him.

Although Graham believed that Nixon would make a better president than Kennedy, he did not want to officially recommend that people vote for Nixon either. Henry Luce, the publisher of *Time* magazine, suggested that Graham write an article describing how he felt about Nixon as a person but not officially supporting him for president. Graham agreed to do this. He had second thoughts after the article was written, however. He didn't want to even come close to suggesting which candidates Christians should support. Luce liked the article and wanted to print it. But Graham convinced him to print instead an article he had written on why every Christian ought to vote in the presidential election. *Time*'s readers liked this article, and Graham avoided endorsing a candidate.

Soon after Kennedy won the election in November 1960, the president-elect called Graham and asked to meet with him. Graham was excited to meet with Kennedy, but he was worried that his friend Nixon would be upset. He called Nixon, who told him, "He's the president-elect. Every time he asks you, you have to go. I would go, so don't think anything of it." Ten days before Kennedy was sworn in as president, Graham appeared at a press conference with him and got his chance to tell the public what he had wanted to say months earlier: "I don't think that Mr. Kennedy's being a Catholic should be held against him by any Protestant. They should judge him on his ability and his character. We should trust and support our new president." Although he had not voted for Kennedy, Graham fully supported his new president. When the news came on November 22, 1963, that President Kennedy had been shot, Graham went on the radio and led a prayer for the president and his family. While he was speaking on the air, he heard that Kennedy had died. Graham waited for a public announcement to be made before beginning a new prayer for Vice President Lyndon Johnson, who would become the new president.

A few weeks after taking office, President Johnson invited Graham to the White House. The two men swam in the White House pool and talked and prayed together for several hours. It turned out that Johnson and Graham had much in common. Johnson's grandfather had been a professor of Bible studies at Baylor University in Texas. The Christian faith was a big part of Johnson's family history and his everyday life. Graham respected Johnson for attending church up to three times a week. When he was elected to a new

Graham (left) and U.S. president Lyndon B. Johnson bow their heads in prayer at a presidential prayer breakfast in Washington, D.C., on February 17, 1966.

term in 1964, Johnson asked Graham to lead the Protestant prayer at a special church service at his inauguration.

CONFLICTS IN THE UNITED STATES

Many social issues were dividing Americans during the 1960s. At the time, African Americans did not enjoy the same personal freedoms and rights that white Americans did. Some people—especially many white southerners—believed that this was the way American society should remain. But many other people, both whites and blacks, worked hard for equal rights for African Americans. As a southern white man, Graham had grown up surrounded by the attitude that African Americans did not deserve equal treatment. But he had also grown up respecting a black man who worked as the foreman on his father's farm. Graham believed that God did not support treating some people badly because of the color of their skin.

Throughout the 1960s, people accused Graham of either supporting the civil rights movement too strongly or not supporting it strongly enough. Graham agreed with Dr. King's methods of using nonviolent demonstrations to bring an end to racism. But Graham wasn't sure how active he should be in the movement. Dr. King told him, "You stay in the stadiums, Billy, because you would have far more impact on the white establishment there than you would if you marched in the streets." Graham agreed with Dr. King's suggestion. He tried to lend his support to the cause of ending racism whenever he could.

In 1965 violence broke out in Selma, Alabama, following a civil rights march. President Johnson personally asked Graham to go to Alabama as a gesture of goodwill between the races. Graham held several rallies around the state that spring, including one at the all-black Tuskegee Institute. Late that summer, riots over racism broke out in the Watts section of Los Angeles. Graham toured the destroyed neighborhood soon after the riots.

Graham addresses a racially integrated audience at his crusade in Birmingham, Alabama, in 1964. Graham had been conducting racially integrated crusades since 1953.

Racism was not the only conflict in the United States during the 1960s. The country was also divided about the Vietnam War (1957–1975). Some Americans felt that the Vietnamese should decide the political direction of their country. They believed that U.S. troops should not be involved in this conflict and should pull out of Vietnam. Others saw this war as a fight against the spread of Communism. As a friend of President Johnson, Graham had heard the president's fears about the war. Johnson told Graham that he thought the United States had to get out of the

Graham addresses troops at Long Binh, Vietnam, in December 1966.

war, but he did not know how to accomplish that. Graham understood the difficult political decisions that needed to be made. He tried to stay out of the decision making. Graham made a trip to Vietnam to preach to troops in 1966. Many people thought that this trip to Vietnam was too political for an evangelist such as Billy Graham. Although Graham insisted that he was trying to stay out of politics, he made several statements supporting the presence of U.S. troops in Vietnam. Some people thought he was allowing Johnson to take advantage of his friendship. Others felt that Graham would say anything, even a statement that he supported the war, in order to get his name in the newspaper.

DIVISION AROUND THE WORLD

Meanwhile, other parts of the world were also being torn apart by political and cultural divisions. At the time, the Union of Soviet Socialist Republics (USSR, or the Soviet Union) included Russia and most of Eastern Europe. The region was under Communist rule. Christians around the world were concerned that people living in Communist countries were not allowed to practice their religion. In 1966 Graham planned a trip to the Communist country of Poland. But twenty-four hours before the BGEA team was scheduled to depart for Poland, they learned that they would be forbidden to enter the country. The Communist government did not want them to preach there. Graham was disappointed. One year later, he was able to visit the Communist country of Yugoslavia. He held

COMMUNISM

Communism is a political and economic system in which the government owns all land and businesses and controls the production and distribution of all goods. Communist governments also do not recognize religions and often do not allow citizens to worship any god. This idea conflicts with the American values of capitalism (where private individuals own land and businesses) and of religious freedom.

two rallies in a large open field near the city of Zagreb (capital of modern-day Croatia) in 1967. Despite pouring rain, more than seven thousand people attended. Some had traveled for several days from other Communist countries including Hungary, Czechoslovakia, and Romania. Graham and the rest of the team were excited by the great reception in a country where worshipping God was severely restricted.

After returning from Eastern Europe, Graham turned his attention to Northern Ireland. For years religious and political differences between Protestants and

Graham preaches in the rain from a podium in a soccer field near Zagreb, Yugoslavia, in 1967.

Catholics had divided that Western European region. Northern Ireland had been under British rule for hundreds of years. Most Protestants supported this arrangement and wanted to remain separate from the predominantly Catholic Republic of Ireland to the south. But many Catholics did not like Great Britain controlling part of Ireland. They wanted a united, independent country. Some violent supporters of this view formed the Irish Republican Army (IRA) and frequently bombed Protestant targets in Northern Ireland. The British army responded with violence, and some parts of Northern Ireland were like a war zone by the early 1970s. Graham was invited to visit Northern Ireland in 1972. He saw the violence firsthand when a bomb exploded in a residential section of Belfast that he was visiting on a Sunday morning.

In 1973 Graham visited South Africa, another country troubled by racial injustice and violence. South Africa's government policy of apartheid kept citizens of different races separate from one another. Graham had been invited to speak in South Africa several times, but he had always refused. Under apartheid he would not be allowed to have racially integrated audiences. But in 1973, Graham was invited to speak to a racially mixed group called the South African Congress on Mission and Evangelism in Durban, South Africa. Graham was happy to speak to this group. But he was more pleased when he learned, after arriving in South Africa, that he would be allowed to hold an interracial crusade as well. He held several evening crusades in March 1973, speaking to a total of more than one hundred thousand black and white South Africans. Graham later said that although he knew that his crusades didn't stop apartheid, spreading God's word was an important first step to healing.

CRISIS IN THE WHITE HOUSE
Richard Nixon and Billy Graham had been friends for several years before Nixon became president. Like President Johnson, President Nixon had a family history of Christian faith. This shared commitment to Christ was the basis for the friendship. In fact, Nixon had committed his life to Jesus at an evangelist rally in Los Angeles as a teenager. During his first term as president, Nixon had often called Graham to pray with him about important issues and crises. But after Nixon was elected to a second term, he faced a crisis so large that even Graham's advice could not help.

The Watergate scandal resulted from a burglary of papers and records from the Democratic National Committee headquarters during Nixon's campaign for reelection. Evidence showed that Nixon had not only been aware of the burglary but had used his power as president to try to cover it up. In 1973 and 1974, the U.S. government investigated Nixon for his role in the burglary and then its cover-up. Rather than face impeachment by the House of Representatives and

U.S. president Richard M. Nixon (standing, front left) *joins Graham at the podium at a crusade in Knoxville, Tennessee, on May 28, 1970.*

removal from office by the Senate, Nixon announced to the public his resignation of the presidency on August 8, 1974. Graham was deeply hurt by the evidence about his friend's criminal behavior. He spoke about the events, calling the Watergate events "sordid," and wrote two articles in the *New York Times*

President Gerald Ford welcomes Billy Graham to the Oval Office for an unofficial visit on April 14, 1975.

about the matter. But he refused to believe that Nixon was a bad person. Instead, he saw him as a good person who had made mistakes. But some Americans were angry that someone with as much influence as Billy Graham did not speak out more strongly against Nixon's actions. Many people thought that Graham had allowed himself to become too close to politics during his friendship with Nixon—something Graham later acknowledged.

After Nixon resigned, Vice President Gerald Ford became president, and Graham and Ford became friends. Many Americans wanted Ford to pardon—

officially excuse from legal punishment—Nixon's participation in Watergate. Graham agreed that pardoning Nixon would be good for the country as a whole and for the former president. He felt that both the country and Nixon needed to get on with life. Along with many others, Graham urged Ford to pardon Nixon, and he did. Again, many people thought that Graham was getting too involved in politics. Graham hoped the pardon would allow the country to begin healing from the wounds of Watergate.

Graham pauses for a photo with his wife, Ruth (left), and his mother, Morrow (right), in 1972 in Charlotte, North Carolina. The occasion is the twenty-fifth anniversary of his first crusade, also held in Charlotte.

Chapter **SIX**

WORLD'S SPIRITUAL LEADER

THE **GRAHAM FAMILY SUFFERED ANOTHER CRISIS IN** 1974. While visiting her daughter Gigi, Ruth decided to string a wire from a roof for her grandchildren to swing on. But while trying to fasten the wire, Ruth fell fifteen feet. She was rushed to a hospital. She had severely damaged her spine and was in a coma—unconscious—for a week. The thought of losing his wife made Graham more aware than ever of the importance of his family.

For years he had felt torn that doing God's work meant he was often absent from his family. All five of the Graham children had struggled with the difficulties and expectations of being a child of such a huge personality. By 1974 his three daughters were all married and committed to a Christian life. But his sons both abused alcohol and were rebellious during their teenage years. Seeing his children struggle pained Graham, and he sometimes wished he had spent more time with them when they were younger. He later wrote, "I . . . have many regrets. For one thing, I would speak less and study more, and I would spend more time with my family. Every day I was absent from my family is gone forever. Although much of that travel was necessary, some of it was not."

Graham tried to carve out more time for his growing family of grandchildren while continuing his evangelical work. His public reputation was as large as ever in the mid-1970s. And in 1976, evangelical Christianity got a huge boost when Jimmy Carter, a born-again Southern Baptist, was elected president of the United States. Carter taught Sunday school and read his Bible daily. He spoke openly to reporters and to the public about his personal faith in Jesus Christ. The Grahams visited with the Carters at the White House. Both were careful to keep some distance between religion and politics. Graham did not want to be criticized again, as he had been after Nixon's presidency, for becoming too close to a political leader.

THE COLD WAR CALLS

In the mid-1970s, Graham felt that his influence was needed around the world. For years, he had spoken out against Communism. He was particularly concerned that Communist governments discouraged people from practicing religions. The United States and its allies (the Western bloc) was involved in a struggle for power with the U.S.S.R. and its allies (the Eastern bloc). This struggle was called the Cold War (1945–1991). No shots were fired, but the struggle for power was worldwide.

Graham had visited the Communist country of Yugoslavia in 1967. He had been waiting since then for a chance to visit other Communist nations to spread the Gospel. In 1977 a Hungarian friend of Graham's helped arrange a trip to Hungary. At the time, the Hungarian government did not completely outlaw religious practice. But churches were given very little power and had to follow many regulations that limited their activities. The Billy Graham Evangelistic Association was able to plan rallies at a few Baptist churches in Hungary. But the organization was not allowed to advertise the visits to the Hungarian people, even at church services. Graham later wrote about an odd experience at his first Hungarian meeting: "At the end of my sermon, I was puzzled by the unfamiliar clicks; for a minute I thought people were gnashing their teeth at me! Instead the sound was, I discovered, from people cutting off their personal tape recorders. This was the case in all the meetings in Hungary: services were being recorded so that the Gospel could be passed all around the country."

During his trip to Hungary, Graham was careful not to offend government leaders. After all, he hoped to be allowed to spread God's word in other Communist countries as well. But he was able to speak with some government leaders. He later reported that one of them admitted to him that the church could be useful in helping to build a united society. At the time, Hungary was known as the Communist country that allowed the most freedom of religion to its citizens. Graham was not certain that he would be invited to some of the stricter Communist nations. The following year, however, he was invited by a group of Polish Protestant churches to visit their country. In 1978 Graham traveled to six Polish cities. As in Hungary, religious services were not allowed on public property, so all meetings had to be held in churches. But the Polish government did allow limited advertising. In one Polish city, Graham even saw a poster advertising his appearance.

COMMUNIST SUPERPOWERS: THE USSR AND CHINA

Graham was pleased with the response he received in Hungary and Poland. He was therefore encouraged to try to visit the biggest Communist power—and the Cold War enemy of the United States—the USSR. In 1982 he was invited to a church-sponsored international peace conference in Moscow, the capital of the USSR. Many people advised Graham not to accept.

They thought that the Soviet government would try to use Graham's presence as proof that he supported Communism and did not support the U.S. government. In fact, Graham remained anti-Communist, but he was determined to spread the word of God inside the USSR. As he told a friend, "Perhaps the Communists in the Soviet Union will try to use me, but I'm also going to use them, to preach the Gospel."

On May 7, 1982, Graham landed in Moscow. Over the next several days, he preached at two Moscow churches and spoke at the peace conference. He was also permitted to hold a press conference and to meet privately with some members of the Soviet government. At one of these meetings, he presented a Soviet official with a list of Soviet citizens known to be in jail due to their political or religious beliefs. Graham asked that the Soviet government release these prisoners. Many Americans said that he should have called publicly for their release. They felt he should have spoken out against other abuses of power by the Soviet government. But Graham felt that if he did that, he would never have been allowed back in the country, nor would he have been taken seriously by the Soviet government.

Back in the United States, Graham continued to speak out against Communism. Some people had accused him of being too soft on Communism during his trip to the Soviet Union. Others accused him of being too strongly anti-Communist. Throughout the 1980s, he supported President Ronald Reagan's attempts to increase U.S.

Graham addresses an audience in Novosibirsk, Siberia, USSR, in September 1984.

strength in the Cold War. He revisited Hungary and
the Soviet Union. He also preached in other Communist countries, including Czechoslovakia, Romania, and East Germany.

But of all the world's Communist powers, China
held a special place in the Grahams' hearts. Ruth
had been born there and lived there with her missionary parents until she was seventeen years old.
She had a deep love for the Chinese people. She
missed the food and customs. China had been a
Communist country since 1949. Ruth had not been
able to return to the land of her birth except for a
brief 1980 visit there with her sister and brother.
But in 1985, Graham received an invitation to
preach in several Chinese churches in September
1987. After two years of negotiations, the trip was
scheduled, only to be postponed at the last minute
by a medical emergency. During a layover in Tokyo
on his way to China, Graham tripped over his brief-
case in his hotel room and broke several ribs. He
had to be flown back to a U.S. hospital and cancel
the long-planned China engagements.

The Grahams worried that their Chinese hosts
would think they had purposely tried to disrupt the
trip. But the Chinese were understanding and
quickly rescheduled the trip for April 1988. After
months of recovery, Graham did travel to China on
April 12, 1988. In seventeen days, the team visited
five Chinese cities and traveled more than two

On their 1988 trip to the People's Republic of China, Graham (front center) and Ruth (front left) accompany Chinese premier Li Peng (front right) on a tour of the Pavilion of Lavender Light in Beijing.

thousand miles. The Grahams spent almost one hour with the Chinese leader, Premier Li Peng. They also visited Ruth's birthplace.

FINAL CHALLENGE: NORTH KOREA

Several Communist governments in Eastern Europe had collapsed in 1989, and the Soviet Union fell apart in 1991. The Cold War was over. By 1992 Communist governments ruled only a small number of countries, including China, North Korea, and Vietnam. Of those, North Korea was the one place Graham had not visited and the last place he expected to preach.

Graham had been to South Korea several times. But the United States and North Korea were still technically at war with each other. The United States and the United Nations (a world peacekeeping organization) had supported South Korea against Communist North Korea during the Korean War (1950–1953). The war had ended with a temporary cease-fire instead of a peace treaty. North Korea still considers the United States to be an enemy. Also, among all Communist countries, North Korea was the least tolerant of religious worship.

But Graham was determined to preach there. He was interested in the country partly because Ruth had gone to boarding school in Korea as a child. And he was saddened to know that thousands of families had been broken apart during the Korean War. Graham hoped to open some communication between North Korea and the rest of the world. In particular, he hoped to lay the groundwork for people in both South Korea and North Korea to see brothers, sisters, parents, and spouses from whom they had been separated for years.

Graham tried every possibility he could think of to gain an invitation to North Korea. Finally, he met the North Korean representative to the United Nations. Soon afterward, the Korean Protestants Federation invited him to visit North Korea in 1992. Since Ruth was ill and unable to travel, Graham's youngest son Ned accompanied him. During this trip, Graham had to be extra careful to stay out of politics. Upon arriving in the capital city of Pyongyang, he told reporters: "I do not come as an emissary [representative] of my government or my nation, but as a citizen of the Kingdom of God."

SLOWING DOWN

The historic North Korean visit was not the only milestone that 1992 held for Graham. That year he returned to Russia to hold his first full-scale crusade there. Unfortunately, a more somber event also occurred that year. During a routine visit to his doctor, Graham was diagnosed with Parkinson's disease. This progressive, incurable disease slowly kills the brain cells that control the body's muscles. Luckily, Graham discovered that he had a type of Parkinson's that progresses slowly. He would likely be able to continue his work for years to come. Nevertheless, the disease slowed him down as he approached his seventy-fourth birthday.

In 1996 Graham had another year of mixed happy and challenging events. On May 2, President Bill Clinton joined congressional leaders in presenting Billy and Ruth with the Congressional Gold Medal, the highest honor Congress can bestow on citizens. The Grahams received the medal for their contributions to morality, racial equality, family, philanthropy, and religion. But that year, Ruth was diagnosed with a life-threatening infection called bacterial spinal

Graham and Ruth celebrated their fiftieth wedding anniversary in 1993. At the anniversary party at the Grahams' home in Montreat, North Carolina (from left to right)*, Gigi, Anne, Ruth (Bunny), Ruth, Graham, Franklin, and Ned pose for a family photograph.*

meningitis. For years she had suffered intense back pain, due in part to her fifteen-foot fall. Four years before the diagnosis, she had undergone surgery to try to contain her pain, but the surgery led to an infection. She underwent another emergency surgery to try to remove the infection. Doctors were not sure that she would survive. But after a week in intensive care in a hospital in North Carolina, she began to improve. Three weeks later, she was able to move home with Billy to Montreat, North Carolina.

By 2000 Billy Graham was also suffering from prostate cancer and often needed a walker to get around. By then both Billy and Ruth had trimmed their schedules dramatically. Their son Franklin took over as chief operating officer and president of the BGEA that year. But Billy Graham continued to travel occasionally across the country to speak and preach.

After the terrorist attacks of September 11, 2001, many people called on Graham to help the United States heal spiritually. On September 14, he addressed the nation from the National Cathedral in Washington, D.C. He told the nation that the destruction of the World Trade Center in New York did not destroy the nation's "spiritual foundation."

FINAL CRUSADES

As Graham's Parkinson's disease progresses, he is less able to carry on with his ministry. Despite his ailing health, however, he continued to hold crusades. In November 2004, he held a four-day crusade in Los Angeles, marking the fifty-fifth anniversary of the 1949 event that made him famous. In June 2005, he led his last crusade, the Greater New York crusade in Flushing Meadows Park, New York. More than 230,000 people attended the New York crusade over three days.

The BGEA continues with the work of Billy Graham, with offices in the United States, Australia, Canada, France, Germany, New Zealand, Spain, and the United Kingdom. *Decision* magazine is published monthly, *The Hour of Decision* radio program is broadcast around the world weekly, and a twenty-four-hour radio ministry called the *Blue Ridge Ministry* is broadcast in seven states daily. The BGEA continues to produce television shows, feature movies, and also spreads the word through "Internet e-vangelism."

After a lifetime of crusades around the world, Graham is finally able to lead an easier, more relaxed life.

BILLY GRAHAM'S HEIR?

I 've been called to the slums of the streets and the ditches of the world."

—Franklin Graham, 1998

As the fourth of Billy Graham's five children and the oldest son, William Franklin Graham III grew up with the world's expectations that he would follow in his father's footsteps. Although Billy Graham was away from home for most of Franklin's childhood in the Appalachian Mountain town of Montreat, North Carolina, it was not easy for Franklin to escape the shadow of his famous father. In his late teens, Franklin rebelled against the image of what people thought Billy Graham's son should be. He grew his hair long, took up smoking, and began drinking heavily.

During his early twenties, Franklin traveled around the world. At the age of twenty-two, alone in a hotel room in Jerusalem, he committed his life to Jesus Christ. Soon afterward, a friend of his father's invited Franklin to join him on a six-week mission to Asia. During that trip, Franklin felt a calling to bring relief to people suffering around the world due to war, famine, disease, and natural disaster. He joined the relief ministry Samaritan's Purse in 1977. One year later, he was elected president of the organization.

In his twenties, Franklin Graham repeatedly said he was not interested in preaching. But in 1989, he conducted his first evangelistic event and committed to spend 10 percent of his time preaching. Each year he conducts at least five festivals (he prefers not to use his father's famous term, *crusade*) around the world as an evangelist for the Billy Graham Evangelistic

Association. Since 1989 he has preached to more than 3.5 million people in cities from Johannesburg, South Africa, to Tupelo, Mississippi.

Franklin has been revered as his father's heir by many, but he has not been without controversy. One month after the September 11, 2001, terrorist attacks, he made some negative public comments about the religion of Islam, saying, "We're not attacking Islam, but Islam has attacked us. The God of Islam is not the same God. He's not the son of God of the Christian or Judeo-Christian faith. It's a different God, and I believe it is a very evil and wicked religion." Franklin Graham has stood behind the remark. However, he did attempt to soften it later in an opinion article for the *Wall Street Journal*. He wrote that while he does not believe Muslims are "evil people because of their faith . . . I decry [disapprove strongly of] the evil that has been done in the name of Islam."

Franklin Graham serves as president and chairman of Samaritan's Purse, headquartered in Boone, North Carolina. The organization has an annual budget of more than $150 million and supports offices in Canada, Australia, the United Kingdom, the Netherlands, and Kenya. It provides relief and assistance in more than one hundred countries worldwide. He also serves as chief operating officer, president, and first vice-chairman of the BGEA. He lives with his wife, Jane, in the mountains near Boone, North Carolina. They have four grown children, William Franklin IV (Will), Roy, Edward, and Jane Austin (Cissie).

Graham preaches at the Adelphia Coliseum during the Nashville, Tennessee, crusade in June 2000. He last led a crusade in New York City in 2005, although he continues to make public appearances as his health permits.

CONTROVERSY

Graham is revered around the world for his work. Many credit him for helping make it acceptable for people to publicly acknowledge their faith. However, his years have not been without controversy. Some people have accused him of allowing public figures to use him in return for publicity. These accusers feel that he has not condemned certain actions, such as alleged abuses of power by Presidents Nixon and Clinton, strongly enough. They charge Graham with being more concerned with his own popularity than with spreading God's word.

A more specific criticism of Graham arose from Graham's relationship with President Nixon. A tape of a conversation between Nixon and Graham was released on which Graham says, "A lot of the Jews are great friends of mine, they swarm around me and are friendly to me because they know I'm friendly with Israel. But they don't know how I really feel about what they are doing to this country. And I have no power, no way to handle them, but I would stand up if under proper circumstances." After the tape was released, Graham apologized for the remarks. Many people believed that he did not realize what he was saying at the time. But others feel that his words damaged his reputation.

HONORS

Billy Graham leaves a legacy as perhaps the best-known preacher of the twentieth century. He has preached to more than 210 million people directly. He has reached millions more through radio, television, and movies. Millions of copies of his books have been sold in thirty-eight languages around the world.

In addition to the Congressional Gold Medal, Graham has been awarded the Templeton Foundation Prize for Progress in Religion and the Ronald Reagan Presidential Foundation Freedom Award for contributions to the cause of faith and freedom. Great Britain made him an honorary knight of the British Empire for his international contributions to civil and religious life over sixty years. He was even inducted into the Gospel Music Hall of Fame, not as a musician but as a supporter of so many new and emerging Christian artists.

Many other groups have honored Graham for his work for individual groups of people. The George Washington Carver Memorial Institute recognized his contributions to improving race relations in the United States. The Anti-Defamation League of the B'nai B'rith and the National Conference of Christians and Jews have also honored him for his efforts to improve relations among people of differing faiths. He also received the Big Brother of the Year Award for his work to help improve the lives of children.

On August 25, 2005, Billy Graham attended the groundbreaking ceremony for the Billy Graham Library in Charlotte, North Carolina. The free library and museum is expected to open in 2007. At the groundbreaking ceremony, Graham used a walker and a hearing aid. He joked about his failing health, saying he needed an interpreter to speak to his wife. He also explained how he has tried to be a leader for people without being political. "People say, are you a Republican? I say I'm like the man in the Civil War who had a gray coat [of the South] and blue trousers [of the North]—and was shot at by both sides."

TIMELINE

1918 William Franklin Graham Jr. is born near Pineville, North Carolina, on November 7.

1934 While still in high school, Billy goes to hear Dr. Mordecai Fowler Ham, a famous evangelist preacher, and commits himself to Jesus Christ.

1936 Billy graduates from high school and enters Bob Jones College in Tennessee.

1937 Billy transfers to the Florida Bible Institute near Tampa, Florida. He preaches his first sermon.

1938 Billy becomes an ordained Baptist minister

1940 Billy graduates from the Florida Bible Institute and enters Wheaton College, near Chicago, Illinois.

1943 Graham graduates from Wheaton College and marries Ruth Bell.

1944 Graham becomes a traveling preacher for Youth for Christ.

1945 The Grahams' first daughter, Gigi, is born.

1946 Graham takes his first trip abroad to preach at Youth for Christ rallies across Europe.

1947 Graham becomes president of Northwestern Schools in Minneapolis, Minnesota.

1948 The Grahams' second daughter, Anne, is born.

1949 Billy Graham holds a citywide campaign in Los Angeles.

1950 Graham hosts the first episode of *The Hour of Decision*, a weekly radio program. The Grahams' third daughter, Ruth, is born.

1951 *Mr. Texas,* the first Billy Graham feature film, is released.

1952 The Grahams' fourth child and first son, William Franklin Graham III, is born.

1954 Graham hosts the Greater London crusade, in London, England, which lasts for three months and attracts more than two million people.

1956 Graham holds crusades in India, Taiwan, the Philippines, Japan, and Korea.

1957 Graham is joined onstage by Martin Luther King Jr. at Graham's New York City crusade.

1958 The Grahams' second son, Nelson (Ned), is born.

1960 Graham preaches across Africa.

1963 Graham prays with Americans on national radio after President John F. Kennedy is shot in Dallas, Texas, on November 22.

1965 Graham leads the Protestant prayer at the inauguration of President Lyndon B. Johnson. Graham holds rallies aimed at decreasing racial tensions in Alabama and Los Angeles.

1967 Graham visits Yugoslavia and holds his first crusade in a Communist country.

1972 Graham visits Northern Ireland, a region torn by civil war.

1973 Graham speaks to a racially mixed group, the South African Congress on Mission and Evangelism, in South Africa.

1974 Ruth Graham falls fifteen feet from a roof and remains unconscious in a coma for a week.

1977 Graham preaches in another Communist country, Hungary.

1982 Graham preaches at churches in Moscow in the Union of Soviet Socialist Republics (USSR).

1988 The Grahams travel to China, where they meet with the Communist country's leader and visit Ruth's childhood village.

1992 Graham preaches in North Korea, a country with which the United States is still technically at war. Graham is also diagnosed with Parkinson's disease.

1996 President Bill Clinton joins congressional leaders in presenting the Grahams with the Congressional Gold Medal, the highest honor Congress can give to individuals. Ruth is hospitalized and undergoes emergency surgery following an infection in her back.

2000 Franklin Graham takes over as chief operating officer and president of BGEA.

2001 Three days after the terrorist attacks of September 11, Graham addresses the nation from the National Cathedral in Washington, D.C.

2004 Graham holds a crusade in Los Angeles fifty-five years after his first crusade in that city made him famous.

2005 In New York City, Graham leads what he says will be his last crusade.

SOURCE NOTES

8–9 Billy Graham, *Just as I Am* (San Francisco: HarperCollins, 1997), 311.

20 Ibid., 25.

21 Ibid., 29.

21 Ibid.

26 Ibid., 40.

27 Ibid., 46.

28 Ibid., 49.

31 William Martin, *A Prophet with Honor: The Billy Graham Story* (Chicago: Quill, 1992), 42.

49 Graham, 149.

49 Ibid., 150.

51 "Sickle for the Harvest," *Time*, November 14, 1949.

53 Graham, 160.

55 Ibid., 178.

59–60 Ibid., 216.

64 Ibid., 265.

71–72 Ibid., 393.

72 Ibid., 402.

75 Ibid., 453.

86 Ibid., 723.

88–89 Ibid., 478.

90 Ibid., 501.

94 Ibid., 622.

98 Ibid., 216.

99 Jeffrey L. Sheler, "All in the Family: As Billy Graham Steps Down, Will His Kids Shape the Future of American Evangelicalism?" *U.S. News & World Report*, December 23, 2002, 4.

99 Ibid.

101 Ibid., 3.

102 Andrea Higgins, "Groundbreaking for Graham Library Precedes 'Living Crusade,'" *Christian Examiner on the Web*, September 11, 2005, http://www.christianexaminer.com/Articles/Articles%20Sep05/Art_Sep05_11.html?

SELECTED BIBLIOGRAPHY:

Bloom, Harold. "Heroes and Icons: Billy Graham." *Time*. June 14, 1999. http://www.time.com/time/time100/heroes/profile/graham01.html (February 27, 2006)

Busby, Russ. *Billy Graham: God's Ambassador*. New York: Time-Life Books, 1999.

Drummond, Lewis. *The Canvas Cathedral: A Complete History of Evangelism from the Apostle Paul to Billy Graham*. Chicago: Nelson Reference, 2002.

Graham, Billy. *Just as I Am*. San Francisco: HarperCollins, 1997.

Leduff, Charlie. "In Time of Turmoil, Graham Offers Soothing Words." *New York Times*, November 20, 2004.

Martin, William. *A Prophet with Honor: The Billy Graham Story*. Chicago: Quill, 1992.

Pollack, John. *Billy Graham: The Authorized Biography*. New York: McGraw-Hill, 1966.

Sheler, Jeffrey L. "All in the Family: As Billy Graham Steps Down, Will His Kids Shape the Future of American Evangelicalism?" *U.S. News & World Report*. December 23, 2002. http://www.usnews.com/usnews/culture/articles/021223/23grahams.htm (February 27, 2006)

Steptoe, Sonja. "Ten Questions for Billy Graham.." *Time*. November 29, 2004. http://www.time.com/time/archive/preview/ 0,10987,995788,00.html (February 27, 2006)

BOOKS BY BILLY GRAHAM

Calling Youth to Christ, Zondervan, 1947

America's Hour of Decision, Van Kampen Press, 1951

I Saw Your Sons at War, Billy Graham Evangelistic Association, 1953

Peace with God, 1st edition,

Doubleday, 1953; revised and expanded, Word Books, 1984

Freedom from the Seven Deadly Sins, Zondervan, 1955

The Secret of Happiness, 1st edition, Doubleday, 1955; revised and expanded, Word Books, 1985

Billy Graham Talks to Teenagers, Zondervan, 1958

My Answer, Doubleday, 1960

Billy Graham Answers Your Questions, World Wide Publications, 1960

World Aflame, Doubleday, 1965

The Challenge, Doubleday, 1969

The Jesus Generation, Zondervan, 1971

Angels: God's Secret Agents, 1st edition, Doubleday, 1975; revised and expanded, Word Books, 1985

How to Be Born Again, Word Books, 1977

The Holy Spirit, Word Books, 1978

Till Armageddon, Word Books, 1981

Approaching Hoofbeats, Word Books, 1983

A Biblical Standard for Evangelists, World Wide Publications, 1984

Unto the Hills, Word Books, 1986

Facing Death and the Life After, Word Books, 1987

Answers to Life's Problems, Word Books, 1988

Hope for the Troubled Heart, Word Books, 1991

Storm Warning, Word Books, 1992

Billy Graham, the Inspirational Writings: Peace with God, the Secret of Happiness, Answers to Life's Problems, Word Books, 1995

Just as I Am: The Autobiography of Billy Graham, Zondervan, 1997

Billy Graham: Three Bestselling Works Complete in One Volume, World Publishing, 2001

Hope for Each Day: Words of Wisdom and Faith, J. Countryman, 2002

The Enduring Classics of Billy Graham, W Publishing Group, 2004

Living in God's Love: The New York Crusade, 2005

The Journey: Living by Faith in an Uncertain World, Thomas W Publishing Group, 2006

FURTHER READING
AND WEBSITES

Gaskins, Pearl. *I Believe In: Christian, Jewish, and Muslim Young People Speak about Their Faith*. Chicago: Cricket Books, 2004.
Read interviews with one hundred teenagers discussing their faith and the symbols, laws, and issues of religions.

Religious Leaders of the World. New York: MacMillian Reference Books, 2000.
Find out about other world religious leaders in encyclopedic entries for biblical, historical, and contemporary figures. Major world religions and religious movements are represented, as are some smaller sects. African and Native American beliefs are also covered.

Sherman, Josepha. *The Cold War*. Minneapolis: Twenty-First Century Books, 2001.
Find out more about the Cold War in this book from the Chronicles of America's Wars series for young adults.

Wooten, Sara McIntosh. *Billy Graham: World Famous Evangelist*. New York: Enslow Publishers, 2001.
Read more about Billy Graham in this biography for teens.

WEBSITES

The Billy Graham Center
http://bgc.gospelcom.net/
This website describes the collections at the Billy Graham Center Museum, on the Wheaton College campus.

Billy Graham Center Archives
http://www.wheaton.edu/bgc/archives/bg.html
The archives section of the Billy Graham Center website features an online chronology of the life of Billy Graham and the BGEA, as well as links to more information.

Billy Graham Evangelistic Association
http://www.billygraham.org/
This website announces crusades and includes audio clips of Billy Graham preaching.

INDEX

Africa, 66, 69, 79, 103; South Africa, 99: apartheid, 79–80
African Americans, 33, 66; and civil rights, 73–74
anti-Semitism, 19–20
Asia, 64, 66, 69, 98

Baptism, 19, 27, 32, 50, 87, 103
Baptist churches, 30, 31, 37, 38, 50, 87
Bible, the, 9, 10, 16, 20, 26, 38, 44; New Testament, 18–19, 87–88; study of, 27, 33, 34, 43, 72
Billy Graham Evangelistic Association (BGEA), 53–54, 59, 62–63, 66, 77, 88, 95–96, 99, 104; publications of, 66, 67, 96

campaigns, 45–48, 54; in Fort Worth, Texas, 57; in London, England, 60–61; in Los Angeles, California, 48, 49, 50–51, 102
Catholicism, 9, 70–72, 78–79
Christ. See Jesus Christ
Cold War, the, 86–93
Communism, 49, 75, 77–78, 87–90; and Billy Graham, 90–94
crusades, 7, 54, 55, 57, 58, 64, 98; Birmingham, Alabama, 75; Charlotte, North Carolina, 84; Europe, Eastern, 77–78, 87–89, 92; final, 96; Jackson, Mississippi, 58; London, England, 10, 58–59, 62; Los Angeles, California, 10, 49, 96; Nashville, Tennessee, 100; New York, 8, 10, 66, 96, 100; Portland, Oregon, 56; Russia, 94; Scotland, 63; South Africa, 78–80; Washington, D.C., 58, 100

evangelism, 54, 58–59, 79; film (movie), 56–57; radio, 37–39, 54–57, 66, 86, 96, 103

God, 10, 25, 78, 94, 99; calling of, 29, 30, 44, 53, 56; commitment to, 20–21, 32, 34, 41, 47, 67, 85; faith in, 18, 42; love of, 20, 47, 53, 64–65, 91–92; will of, 61, 74; word of, 10, 66, 80, 90, 100; worship of, 77, 78, 94
Graham, Billy. See Graham, William Franklin Jr., (Billy)
Graham, Morrow Coffey (mother), 12, 14, 16–17, 18, 20, 27, 84
Graham, Nelson Edman, (Ned) (son), 67, 68, 94, 95, 103
Graham, Ruth Bell (wife), 38, 40–42, 56, 61, 68, 84, 86, 92–93, 95; and bacterial spinal meningitis, 94, 104; birthplace, 91–92, 104;

education of, 34, 37; honors, 94; injury of, 85, 104; marriage of, 36, 37, 95, 103
Graham, Ruth Bell, (Bunny) (daughter), 56, 68, 85, 94
Graham, Virginia (Gigi) Leftwich (daughter), 42, 61, 85, 95, 103
Graham, William Franklin, (Frank) (father), 12, 14, 18–20, 21, 23, 25, 74
Graham, William Franklin Jr., (Billy): baptism of, 21, 31; birth and childhood, 14–15; ; commitment to Jesus Christ, 20–22; and Communism, 89—94; early resistance to religion, 18–20; education of, 22–24, 25–29, 33–35, 37, 39–40, 46, 103; fame and honors of, 6, 10, 11, 45–55, 94; health of, 72, 94–96, 101–102, 104; marriage, 34–37, 95; media attention of, 6, 7, 39, 47–49, 59, 76, 96; message of, 7–10, 31, 47, 53, 62–65; and Northwestern Schools, 43–44; ordination of, 32, 103; and September 11 (2001) terrorist attacks, 96, 104; and U.S. social issues, 73–76. *See also*, African Americans: and civil rights; Billy Graham Evangelistic Association; campaigns; crusades; evangelism; politics and political strife; Youth for Christ
Graham, William Franklin III

(son), 58, 95, 103; as heir, 98–99
Ham, Mordecai Fowler, 19–22, 103

Jesus Christ: commitment to, 9–10, 20–23, 80, 98, 103; faith in, 87; as savior, 8; second coming of, 18–19

King, Martin Luther, Jr., 67, 103. *See also* African Americans: and civil rights

Minder, John, 24, 27, 29–30

politics and political strife, 69, 75, 76, 83, 87, 107; global division, 77–80; Northern Ireland, 78–79, 104; and North Korea, 92–94, 104; and Union of Soviet Socialist Republics (USSR, Soviet Union), 77, 87, 90–92, 104; Vietnam War, 75–76
presidents, U.S.: Carter, Jimmy, 86; Clinton, Bill, 94; Ford, Gerald, 82–83; Kennedy, John F., 69–72; Johnson, Lyndon B., 69, 72–73; Nixon, Richard M., 80–82, 86
Protestantism, 9, 10, 72, 73, 78–79, 88, 94, 102

Shea, George Beverly (Bev), 39, 45–46

Youth for Christ (YFC), 40–46, 55, 103

OTHER TITLES FROM LERNER AND BIOGRAPHY®:

Ariel Sharon
Arnold Schwarzenegger
The Beatles
Benito Mussolini
Benjamin Franklin
Bill Gates
Billy Graham
Carl Sagan
Che Guevara
Chief Crazy Horse
Colin Powell
Daring Pirate Women
Edgar Allan Poe
Eleanor Roosevelt
Fidel Castro
Frank Gehry
George Lucas
George W. Bush
Gloria Estefan
Hillary Rodham Clinton
Jacques Cousteau
Jane Austen
Jesse Ventura
J. K. Rowling
Joseph Stalin
Latin Sensations

Legends of Dracula
Legends of Santa Claus
Malcolm X
Mao Zedong
Mark Twain
Maya Angelou
Mohandas Gandhi
Napoleon Bonaparte
Nelson Mandela
Osama bin Laden
Pope Benedict XVI
Queen Cleopatra
Queen Elizabeth I
Queen Latifah
Rosie O'Donnell
Saddam Hussein
Stephen Hawking
Thurgood Marshall
Tiger Woods
Tony Blair
Vladimir Putin
Wilma Rudolph
Winston Churchill
Women in Space
Women of the Wild West
Yasser Arafat

ABOUT THE AUTHOR

Sandy Donovan has written many books for young readers, including *The Channel Tunnel, How a Bill Becomes a Law, Budgeting,* and a biography of President James Buchanan. She lives in Minneapolis, Minnesota, with her husband and two sons.

PHOTO ACKNOWLEDGMENTS

The images in this book are used with the permission of: Lyndon B. Johnson Library photo by Yoichi R. Okamoto, pp. 2, 73; © 1957 Newsweek, Inc. All rights reserved. Reprinted by permission. Photo courtesy of The Billy Graham Evangelistic Association, p. 6; © AP/Wide World Pictures, pp. 8, 90; The Billy Graham Evangelistic Association, pp. 12, 15, 19, 22, 24, 36, 41, 43, 45, 60, 68, 75, 76, 78, 92, 95; Florida State Archives, p. 29; © Loomis Dean//Time Life Pictures/Getty Images, p. 48; Library of Congress, p. 49 (LC-USZ62-83833); © Hulton Archive/Getty Images, p. 50; Norton & Peel, Minnesota Historical Society, p. 52; © Todd Strand/Independent Picture Service, p. 57; © Bettmann/CORBIS, pp. 63, 65, 84; John F. Kennedy Presidential Library and Museum, p. 70; National Archives (#194319), p. 81; Gerald R. Ford Presidential Library, p. 82; © Bryan Smith/ZUMA Press, pp. 97, 100.

Front cover: © David Hume Kennerly/Getty Images.
Back cover: The Billy Graham Evangelistic Association.

WEBSITES
Website addresses in this book were valid at the time of printing. However, because of the nature of the Internet, some addresses may have changed or sites may have closed since publication. While the author and Publisher regret any inconvenience this may cause readers, no responsibility for any such changes can be accepted by the author or Publisher.